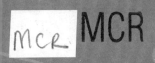

Electromagnetism

by Elizabeth R. Cregan

Science Contributor
Sally Ride Science
Science Consultants
Michael E. Kopecky, Science Educator
Jane Weir, Physicist

MISSION: SCIENCE

Sally Ride Science

Developed with contributions from Sally Ride Science™

Sally Ride Science™ is an innovative content company dedicated to fueling young people's interests in science.

Our publications and programs provide opportunities for students and teachers to explore the captivating world of science—from astrobiology to zoology.

We bring science to life and show young people that science is creative, collaborative, fascinating, and fun.

To learn more, visit www.SallyRideScience.com

First hardcover edition published in 2010 by
Compass Point Books
151 Good Counsel Drive
P.O. Box 669
Mankato, MN 56002-0669

Editor: Robert McConnell
Designer: Heidi Thompson
Editorial Contributor: Sue Vander Hook

Art Director: LuAnn Ascheman-Adams
Creative Director: Joe Ewest
Editorial Director: Nick Healy
Managing Editor: Catherine Neitge

 This book was manufactured with paper containing at least 10 percent post-consumer waste.

Library of Congress Cataloging-in-Publication Data
Cregan, Elizabeth R.
  Electromagnetism / by Elizabeth R.C. Cregan.—1st hardcover ed.
     p. cm.—(Mission: Science)
  Includes index.
  ISBN 978-0-7565-4226-9 (library binding)
  1. Electromagnetism—Juvenile literature. I. Title. II. Series.
  QC760.2.C74 2010
  537—dc22   2009002769

Visit Compass Point Books on the Internet at *www.compasspointbooks.com*
or e-mail your request to *custserv@compasspointbooks.com*

Table of Contents

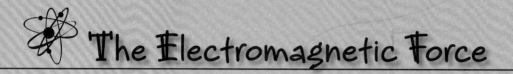

The Electromagnetic Force

You may not know it, but you use electromagnets many times every day. They come in many forms, but all electromagnets use electrical energy and magnetism. Magnetism is an object's ability to attract iron and other materials. Electromagnetic devices combine these two powerful forces to do a lot of important things.

Electromagnets help produce electricity for homes and businesses. They send a signal to your computer every time you press a key. Electromagnets run electric motors and generators that create electricity. They bring pictures to TV screens. Nearly everything we do is affected by electromagnets. Without them, the world would be very different.

Lodestone attracts iron and some other materials.

Did You Know?

The mineral lodestone, also known as magnetite, was common in Magnesia, a region in Greece. The word *magnet* comes from a Greek word meaning "stone of Magnesia."

▲ Benjamin Franklin believed lightning would go down a kite string.

People have always been curious about magnetism and electricity. The ancient Chinese and Greeks saw magnetism at work in a mineral called lodestone. Lodestone is a natural magnet that attracts small pieces of iron.

In 1752 Benjamin Franklin, with his son William, flew a kite in a thunderstorm as an experiment. Lightning went down the kite string to a key Franklin had attached to the string. When he touched the key, he felt the electricity.

Atoms at Work

How does electromagnetism work? The story begins with nature's building block, the atom. Everything in nature is made of matter. Matter is made of extremely tiny particles called atoms, which are made of even smaller particles.

At the center of each atom is a nucleus. Inside the nucleus are very tiny particles called protons and neutrons. Protons have positive electrical charges. Neutrons have no charge.

Swirling around the nucleus are clouds of very small particles called electrons. Electrons carry a negative charge. Normally an atom has the same number of electrons and protons, which makes it electrically neutral. It is the attraction of these opposite charges to each other that holds the atom together.

Some atoms' electrons can break free of the atoms and join other atoms. As the electrons jump from atom to atom, a flow of electricity is happening.

← Electrons moving through a material, such as an electric wire, create an electrical current. The current can be used to provide power.

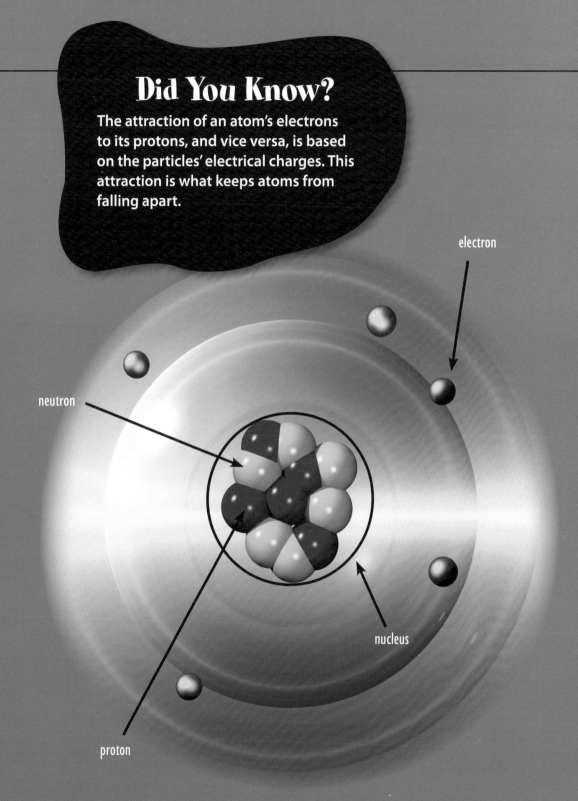

The attraction of an atom's electrons to its protons, and vice versa, is based on the particles' electrical charges. This attraction is what keeps atoms from falling apart.

electron

neutron

nucleus

proton

Electricity

Let's take a closer look at electricity. There are two types: static electricity, which is not moving, and dynamic electricity, which is moving and is also called an electrical current.

Static electricity is so easy to make that you can do it without thinking about it. Shuffle your feet across a carpet. Then touch your friend's hand. You might both feel a small shock. This shock is a tiny jolt of static electricity.

What's happening? When you rub your feet on a carpet, you transfer electrons from the carpet to your feet or shoes. The loss and gain of electrons gives one surface a positive charge and the other a negative charge.

This difference between these charges is called a potential difference. When you touch your friend's hand, the jolt you feel is the electrons moving from one hand to the other. This

A touch is all it takes to experience static electricity.

eliminates the potential difference and makes both surfaces neutral again.

An electrical current is the flow of electrically charged particles—usually electrons—from one place to another. For a current to flow, there must be some kind of conductor—something through which electrons can move. Many things, even liquids, can be conductors. Many metals are good conductors, but so is water.

A current also requires an electrical circuit. A circuit is a closed loop of conducting material that the electricity can flow through. If the loop is broken, the electricity stops flowing. When you unplug a lamp, you break the lamp's circuit, and the lamp is turned off.

Did You Know?

In the 19th century, sweethearts enjoyed sharing what were called electric kisses. They would shuffle their feet across a rug and then kiss. The kiss included a small jolt of static electricity.

Magnetism

Now let's look at magnetism, the other part of electromagnetism. Magnetism is an invisible force—a push or a pull—that affects only certain things. One of those things is iron. Magnetic force can move a piece of iron even without touching it.

Magnetism can reach only so far, though. The reach of a magnet is called its magnetic field. Magnetic forces can be felt within the field but not outside it. A magnetic field is made of invisible lines of force. The lines go from one end of the magnet to the other end. The two ends are called the north and south poles of the magnet.

If you place the north pole of a magnet next to the south pole of another magnet, something interesting happens. The invisible magnetic fields pull on each other. Each pole is attracted to the other. They can easily stick together. But if you put the north pole of

Magnetic Facts

- The field lines of a magnet go from the north pole to the south pole.

- Magnetic force is strongest at a magnet's ends.

- Magnetic force is stronger close to a magnet and weaker farther away from it.

- If you cut a magnet in half, each piece becomes a magnet, with its own north and south poles.

The magnetic fields of magnets can be seen by sprinkling iron filings around them. The iron filings line up along the lines of force.

one magnet next to the north pole of another magnet, the magnets move apart. The magnetic fields of the two north poles are pushing against each other.

Did You Know?

When the ancient Chinese tied a string around a piece of lodestone and let the stone hang, it pointed toward the north. The lodestone acted as a compass. Chinese military leaders were probably the first to figure out directions using compasses.

A Big Magnet

A magnet's north and south poles are attracted to the north and south poles of Earth. Yes, Earth's poles are like the poles of a magnet. Earth has a huge magnetic field, as if a giant bar magnet were running through its center. But what we call Earth's north pole actually behaves like a magnet's south pole. That means a magnet's north pole is attracted to it.

The first known magnets were natural ones, such as lodestone. Scientists began to wonder whether they could make magnets themselves. In 1820 a Danish scientist named Hans Ørsted found a way.

When he placed a compass near an electrical current, he noticed that the needle on the compass moved. The electrical current had created a magnetic field. When Øersted investigated further, he found that a current in a wire produces a magnetic field that goes around the wire.

This was a very important discovery. It showed that there is a close relationship between electricity and magnetism. That knowledge led to the discovery of the electromagnet, which changed people's lives.

A simple electromagnet can be made by attaching a coil of wire to the negative and positive ends of a battery. Electrons flow from the negative end of the battery, through the coiled wire, to the battery's positive end. This current of electricity creates a small magnetic field around the wire.

An electromagnet can be made stronger either by putting more turns or more wires in the coil or by increasing the current in the circuit. Putting a piece of soft iron like a nail through the coil makes the electromagnet even stronger. With all electromagnets, when the current stops, the magnetic effect does, too.

Electromagnets can be created in many ways. Some early electromagnets contained a coil of wire attached to the negative and positive ends of a battery.

Electromagnets Move Motors

At the heart of every electric motor is an electromagnet. When you put magnets next to each other, magnetic forces act between them so that the magnets either push away from each other or attract each other. Electric motors use these forces to create a rotating motion. The rotating motion can be used to power everything from electric fans to vacuum cleaners to vehicles.

Invisible Lines of Force

In the 1830s, English scientist Michael Faraday wondered how electricity and magnetism were related. Faraday liked to test scientific ideas with experiments. His work proved that electricity and magnetism were really parts of the same thing—what he called a "single unified force." He called this force electromagnetism.

▲ Michael Faraday (1791–1867)

Faraday's ideas probably led others to use electricity in their inventions. His ideas were very important in the invention of the dynamo. It was the first electrical generator. Using magnetism to produce electricity, a dynamo could provide enough power to make machines work.

Did You Know?

The idea behind Faraday's generator is used to make electricity for bicycle lights. The energy produced by pedaling the bike is changed into electrical current by a small generator on one of the bike's wheels. Wires connect the generator to the lights.

The dynamo was invented in 1832. A simple dynamo
could make electricity using muscle power.

Generators Get Electricity Flowing

What exactly is an electrical generator, and how does it work? A generator converts energy from other sources into electrical energy. This energy is what makes a light or a television work when it is switched on. When the energy is made, electricity and magnetism are at work. To better understand what these forces do, let's take a look at how an electrical current and electromagnetism are made.

Electricity needs a conductor to move it from one point to another. Materials that are good conductors have electrons that move easily. Copper wire is a good conductor. Aluminum, gold, and silver are also sometimes used as conductors. But electricity also needs something to make it move through the conductor. Generators are often used to do this.

Generators create electricity.

Did You Know?

Generators change mechanical energy into electrical energy. Where does the mechanical energy come from? In many power plants, it comes from the chemical energy in coal. Burning coal creates heat energy. The heat is used to boil water and make steam. When the steam turns the blades of a machine, heat energy changes to mechanical energy. The mechanical energy runs the generator.

We know that an electrical current moving through a wire creates a magnetic field. Generators work in the opposite way. A generator uses magnets to create an electrical current in a conducting wire. As it continues to create a current, the generator produces a steady flow of electricity in the form of electrons moving in the wire.

Imagine a pipe, but pretend that it's a conducting wire. The pipe is filled with ping-pong balls. Pretend the balls are electrons. What happens if you push one more ball into the end of the filled pipe? All the balls move along the pipe and bump the last one out the other end. Electrons move this way along a wire and into an electrical appliance.

Electrons travel along the red wire to the bulb.

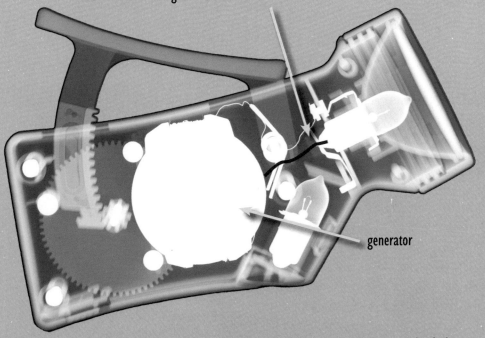

generator

An X-ray of a hand-crank flashlight shows how the mechanical energy of pushing the handle powers the generator. As the parts of the generator turn, it creates electrical energy for the lightbulb.

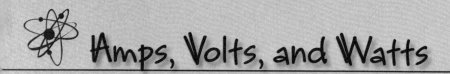

Amps, Volts, and Watts

When a generator pushes electricity through a wire, two things happen. The generator pushes a certain number of electrons through the wire. The amount of this current is measured in amps, which is short for amperes. The pressure that the generator puts on the electrons is a force that is measured in volts.

Think about how these ideas might be related to your home or school building. Power outlets deliver a certain amount of volts to an electrical device. The current flow from the outlet to the device is measured in amps.

Amps and volts are put together to figure out how much power is being used. This is measured in watts. Watts are found by multiplying the amps and volts together. That tells you how many electrons are moving and how much force is behind the electrons.

Each lightbulb has a certain number of watts, depending on how bright it is. A 100-watt bulb makes a lot more light than a 40-watt bulb, but it also uses a lot more electricity. Compact fluorescent lightbulbs use much less power to produce the same amount of light.

Did You Know?

Annie Easley is a scientist who works with batteries. But these are not just any batteries. She develops computer codes to help NASA find the best and longest-lasting batteries for the electric-powered vehicles used in space.

Did You Know?

The volt is named for Alessandro Volta of Italy. He invented one of the first electric batteries in 1799. The watt is named for James Watt, who improved the steam engine. Watts measure power in machines as well as in electrical currents.

Power for Tunes

The battery in your digital music player is a chemical battery. The chemicals in it work together to release electrons. Those are captured to create an electrical current. The electrons leave the battery, flow through the music player's circuit, and then return to the battery. Many iPods and other digital music players use lithium-ion batteries. They contain lithium, a metal that can store a lot of energy. Lithium-ion batteries can be recharged hundreds of times to keep them fully powered and ready to play music. Lithium-ion batteries are also used in cell phones and laptop computers.

After Thomas Edison perfected the lightbulb in 1879, he began working to send electricity into people's homes. He also promised to light the entire city of New York. There was a problem, though. The electricity then used in homes was direct current, or DC for short. Direct current always flows in one direction.

DC was a poor choice for sending electricity long distances because a lot of voltage was lost in the cables it went through. There was no good way to increase DC voltage before the electricity was sent or to reduce the voltage at the other end.

So Edison had a big problem. But Nikola Tesla, who worked for him, had an idea for solving it. He wanted to use another kind of current, alternating current, or AC. This kind of current reverses direction many times in one second. Its voltage could be boosted and reduced much more easily than DC voltage, so AC was the better choice for sending electricity over long distances.

The Electric Highway

A circuit is a path that an electrical current follows as it moves through a conductor, such as a copper wire. All circuits have a power source. They also need a load, such as a light, and a way for electricity to travel to and from the source, such as wires.

Circuits must be unbroken in order to work. If there is a break in the conductor, the electricity can't get through. When you flip a light's switch off, you are breaking its circuit, and the bulb goes out.

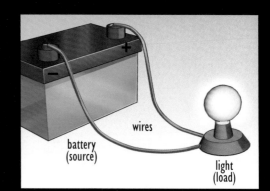

wires

battery
(source)

light
(load)

Edison and Tesla disagreed about which kind of current to use. But Tesla's idea worked best. Today alternating current is the electricity that comes from power plants and is used in most homes and businesses.

A transformer is used to raise or lower AC voltage. ⬇

Changing Power

The world uses more than one kind of AC power. The electricity used in the United States changes direction, and then reverses itself, 60 times per second. Europe's AC changes direction 50 times per second. A U.S. electrical device might not work in other countries for this reason and because of voltage differences. An adapter may be needed to make it work.

Did You Know?

AC electricity can travel long distances because of transformers. Transformers increase or decrease voltage. Voltage has to be increased for long-distance delivery of electric power. At the receiving end, transformers are used to reduce the voltage to a safe level for customers.

Inventions that use electricity and magnetism have greatly improved our ways of communicating with each other.

The telegraph was the first practical use of electricity. In 1844 Samuel F.B. Morse created the first telegraph line. The line connected Washington, D.C., to Baltimore, Maryland. Morse's telegraph was a very simple device. It used a battery, a switch, and a small electromagnet to send bursts of electricity through a wire. He invented a code, called Morse code, to communicate through the telegraph wires.

The telegraph made a big difference in Americans' lives. It was used to send news over long distances, and both armies used it during the Civil War. But people also wanted to hear the voices of loved ones who lived far away. They got their wish in 1875, when Alexander Graham Bell invented the telephone. Now the world could communicate in a more natural way over long distances.

Railroad Communication

To keep trains running safely, the railroads needed a way to communicate, so they used the telegraph. Mattie "Ma" Kiley was one of the first female telegraphers to work for the railroads. Dispatchers, who controlled train movements, used the telegraph to send messages back and forth. Kiley worked in railroad telegraphy until 1942, when she retired.

Dots and Dashes

Morse code is a special language of dots (short electric signals) and dashes (longer signals). It was designed for the telegraph, but it was later used with radios. Certain combinations of dots and dashes represent certain letters of the alphabet. Here is how the international signal for help, the letters S O S, would be sent using Morse code: ••• — — — •••

A •—	N —•	0 —————
B —•••	O ———	1 •————
C —•—•	P •——•	2 ••———
D —••	Q ——•—	3 •••——
E •	R •—•	4 ••••—
F ••—•	S •••	5 •••••
G ——•	T —	6 —••••
H ••••	U ••—	7 ——•••
I ••	V •••—	8 ———••
J •———	W •——	9 ————•
K —•—	X —••—	Fullstop •—•—•—
L •—••	Y —•——	Comma ——••——
M ——	Z ——••	Query ••——••

Using a telegraph, operators could send messages very quickly. ▽

Electromagnetism is the force behind all electronic devices, including many communication tools. The personal computer and the cell phone are two examples. These devices keep getting smaller because the parts that make them run have become tiny. Two of those parts are called transistors and microchips.

Transistors are used in electronic devices to control and strengthen electrical currents. Scientists and engineers have learned how to make transistors smaller and even more powerful.

They have also learned how to create entire electrical circuits on small pieces of silicon known as microchips. Silicon is a nonmetallic material that is easy to find. It makes up nearly one-third of Earth's crust.

The first microchip was about half an inch wide. Today some chips are much smaller than that. Their tiny size lets them easily fit in such devices as laptop computers, cell phones, and digital music players. The circuits on these chips are so small that you would need a microscope to see them.

Tiny transistors line up on a microchip.

Solar Energy

Using the power of the sun is one of the best ways to make electricity. Solar panels are made of a thin layer of a semiconductor, such as silicon, and thin strips of metal. A semiconductor is a material that carries electricity, but not as well as a conductor. When sunlight hits the panel, the silicon absorbs it. Electrons are knocked loose and flow freely. The electrons are captured to create electricity.

Peering Into the Future

Scientists and engineers will continue to find new ways to use electromagnetism. Lasers are one example of what they are doing with it today. A laser beam is a concentrated stream of light energy. Lasers rely on the power of electromagnetism. Scientists discovered a way to use the energy in atoms to make lasers.

Lasers are already being used in many ways. Doctors use them to operate on patients. The grocery clerk uses a laser to scan your cereal and milk packages at the checkout counter. You use lasers when you listen to a CD player—a tiny laser plays the music stored on the compact disc. But you can expect to see even more exciting uses of lasers in the future.

Electromagnetism has changed how we live every day. From kite experiments to laser beams, we have learned a lot about using electricity and magnetism to power our world.

Did You Know?

People who can't see well have a chance to do so now, thanks to Dr. Patricia Bath. The ophthalmologist developed a device called a laserphaco probe. It uses a laser beam to remove cataracts from the eye. Cataracts cause blurry vision and even blindness.

Some extremely tiny circuits combine ▷ living parts, such as human nerve cells, with nonliving parts.

Magnets Let Doctors See Inside the Body

Doctors often use magnetic resonance imaging to find out whether something is wrong with a patient. They don't have to cut open the patient to look. They can see inside the body with MRI. It works by using a powerful magnet. The magnet makes hydrogen atoms in the body behave in a way that lets parts of the body be seen.

The magnet in an MRI scanner is so powerful that metal objects can't be taken into the same room with it. Normally harmless things such as paper clips and pens become dangerous when the scanner is turned on. They can be pulled by the strong magnetic power and fly toward the patient. The patient lies in the center of the scanner, where the magnet has its greatest power. Even something as heavy as a metal pipe would be pulled from your hands if you stood near the MRI machine.

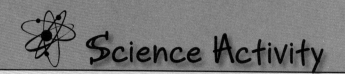

Create an Electromagnet

Electrical currents have magnetic fields around them. When you make a coil out of conducting wire, you strengthen the magnetic field. This device is an electromagnet. The more coils in the wire, the stronger the magnetic field. Adding a piece of metal makes the electromagnet even stronger.

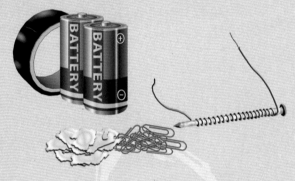

Materials

- 2-inch (5-centimeter) iron nail

- heavy, insulated wire

- two D-cell batteries

- 10 paper clips

- scraps of paper

- masking tape

Procedure

1   Wrap the wire around the nail 20 times.

2   Leave about 8 inches (20 cm) of wire hanging from each end of the coil

3 Peel back 3 inches (8 cm) of the insulation material from each end of the wire

4 Tape the positive end of one battery to the negative end of the other battery so they are in a line.

5 Tape one end of the wire to the positive end of the batteries and one end to the negative end.

6 Make a pile of paper clips and a pile of paper scraps.

7 Run the nail with the coiled wire over the paper clips and the scraps of paper. Observe what happens.

8 Try steps 1 through 7 again, but this time wrap the wire around the nail 50 times.

9 Make another pile of paper clips.

10 Run the nail with the coiled wire over the paper clips. Observe what happens.

11 Record your results.

Which makes a better electromagnet, more electricity or more coils around the nail? To find out, do an experiment using extra batteries.

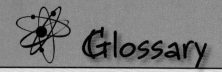

Glossary

alternating current (AC)—electrical current that changes direction many times a second

ampere (amp)—unit of measurement of the amount of an electrical current

atom—smallest particle of an element

battery—device that uses chemicals to produce electricity

circuit—path that an electrical current follows as it moves through a conductor

compass—device used to determine direction (north, south, east, or west)

conductor—material through which electricity can move easily; most conductors are metals

direct current (DC)—electrical current that always moves in the same direction

electrical current—flow of electrically charged atomic particles, usually electrons, from one place to another

electricity—electrically charged atomic particles, usually electrons, that are moving or can move

electromagnetism—magnetic force produced by an electrical current

electromagnet—temporary magnet made of a wire carrying an electrical current; usually the wire is coiled around a piece of iron

electron—negatively charged particle that moves outside the nucleus of an atom

generator—machine that changes mechanical energy into electrical energy

laser—device that creates a powerful, narrow beam of light

lodestone—mineral with natural magnetic properties

magnetic field—region in which a magnetic force acts

magnetism—property of magnets that allows them to attract certain materials, such as iron

magnet—natural or artificial object that can attract certain materials, such as iron

microchip—very small electronic device containing extremely small electronic circuits

NASA—National Aeronautics and Space Administration, which runs the U.S. space program

neutron—particle in the nucleus of an atom; it has no electrical charge

nucleus—dense center of an atom, made of protons and neutrons

ophthalmologist—doctor who specializes in care of the eyes

proton—positively charged particle in the nucleus of an atom

static electricity—electrical charge that collects on the surface of objects, often when they rub against something

telegraph—electrical device that can send messages over a wire

transformer—device that increases or decreases the voltage of alternating electrical current

transistor—device used to control or strengthen electrical current in electronic equipment

volt—unit for measuring the force of an electrical current or the stored power of a battery

watt—unit for measuring the power of an electrical current

André Marie Ampère (1775–1836)
French physicist and mathematician who determined that electric currents produce magnetic fields; current strength is measured in amperes in his honor

Peter Joseph William Debye (1884–1966)
Dutch-American physicist who studied the distribution of electric charges in molecules

Michael Faraday (1791–1867)
English physicist and chemist who proposed the idea of magnetic lines of force, developed the first electrical generator, and pioneered the study of low temperatures

Sir John Ambrose Fleming (1849–1945)
British physicist and electrical engineer who invented the vacuum tube, used to create and change electrical signals

Benjamin Franklin (1706–1790)
American scientist, inventor, politician, and philosopher who experimented with electricity; defined negative and positive charges

Werner Karl Heisenberg (1901–1976)
German physicist who developed the uncertainty principle, which advanced modern physics; determined that the atomic nucleus consists of protons and neutrons

Joseph Henry (1797–1878)
American physicist who invented the large-scale electromagnet, the electric relay used in the telegraph, and the electric motor

Heinrich Rudolf Hertz (1857–1894)
German physicist who discovered radio waves and determined their velocity; the hertz, the unit used to measure frequency, was named in his honor

Robert Hofstadter (1915–1990)
American physicist who discovered the structures of protons and neutrons

Sir Joseph Larmor (1857–1942)
Irish physicist who was one of the first to develop a theory explaining the magnetic fields of Earth and the sun

James Clerk Maxwell (1831–1879)
British physicist whose math equations were a basis for understanding electromagnetism; determined that light is electromagnetic radiation

Georg Simon Ohm (1787–1854)
German physicist who found that electrical current is equal to the ratio of the voltage to the resistance, which is known as Ohm's law

Sir Owen Willans Richardson (1879–1959)
British physicist who explained the Edison effect, in which heated metals give off electrons

Ernst August Friedrich Ruska (1906–1988)
German physicist who determined that a magnetic coil can focus a beam of light; developed the first electron microscope

William Sturgeon (1783–1850)
British physicist who invented the electromagnet

Nikola Tesla (1856–1943)
Serbian-American inventor who discovered the principles of alternating currents and developed the first AC motor and the Tesla coil, a type of transformer; magnetic field strength is measured in teslas in his honor

Alessandro Volta (1745–1827)
Italian physicist who built the first chemical battery and was the first to produce and work with electrical currents; the force of electricity is measured in volts in his honor

Sir Charles Wheatstone (1802–1875)
British physicist who developed the first commercial electric telegraph; developed a device for measuring electrical resistance

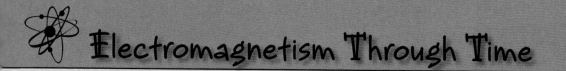

450 B.C. Leucippus, of Miletus, a city in ancient Greece, introduces the idea of the atom

1492 A.D. Christopher Columbus notices that a magnetic compass points in different directions at different longitudes

1747 Benjamin Franklin discovers that a conductor can draw an electric charge from a charged body and invents the lightning rod

1749 The first artificial magnet is developed by British physicist and teacher John Canton

1751 Franklin distinguishes between positive and negative electrical charges

1791 Italian physician and physicist Luigi Galvani determines that when different metals touch in a frog's muscle, an electrical current is produced

1800 Alessandro Volta creates a method for storing electricity

1819 Danish physicist Hans Christian Ørsted discovers electromagnetism

1820 André Marie Ampère formulates the first laws of electromagnetism

1823 William Sturgeon develops the first electromagnet

1830s Michael Faraday experiments with electricity and magnetism, proves they are a "single unified force," and calls the force electromagnetism

1873	James Clerk Maxwell explains electro-magnetism and determines that radio waves must exist
1888	Heinrich Hertz detects and produces radio waves
1895	German physicist Wilhelm Röntgen discovers X-rays
1897	British physicist Sir Joseph Thomson discovers the electron
1911	New Zealand physicist Ernest Rutherford discovers the proton
1913	Danish physicist Niels Bohr determines the basic structure of the atom
1951	The first electricity is generated from a nuclear breeder reactor
1960	American physicist Theodore Maiman produces the first working laser
1973	The first magnetic resonance image is made
1977	Magnetic resonance imaging is first performed on a human
1990	A group of American scientists says a powerful gun using a series of magnetic fields could be used to launch small satellites into orbit at very low cost
2008	The U.S. Food and Drug Administration approves a treatment for depression that uses magnets to produce electrical currents in the brain and stimulate nerve cells

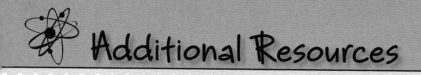

Burgan, Michael. *Nikola Tesla: Physicist, Inventor, Electrical Engineer.* Mankato, Minn.: Compass Point Books, 2009.

Carlson, Laurie. *Thomas Edison for Kids: His Life and Ideas: 21 Activities.* Chicago: Chicago Review Press, 2006.

Dreier, David. *Electrical Circuits: Harnessing Electricity.* Minneapolis: Compass Point Books, 2008.

Parker, Steve. *The Science of Electricity and Magnetism: Projects and Experiments With Electrons and Magnets.* Chicago: Heinemann Library, 2005.

Riley, Peter. *Electricity and Power.* North Mankato, Minn.: Smart Apple Media, 2006.

Internet Sites

FactHound offers a safe, fun way to find Internet sites related to this book. All of the sites on FactHound have been researched by our staff.

Here's all you do:

Visit *www.facthound.com*

FactHound will fetch the best sites for you!

Index

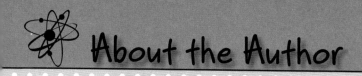

Elizabeth R. Cregan

Elizabeth R. Cregan is a freelance writer living in Jamestown, Rhode Island. She enjoys writing about a wide variety of topics for children and young adults, including science, natural history, current events, and biography. She has a bachelor of science degree in special education and a master's degree in distance education. She is also the owner of Cregan Associates, a consulting firm specializing in grant and technical writing.

Image Credits